T0284433

DRAGON QUEEN

a guide

CHRISTINE R. DOWNS

DRAGON QUEEN

A guide

©2024 Christine R. Downs

Hard Cover ISBN: 979-8-35094-300-9
Soft Cover ISBN: 979-8-35096-658-9
eBook ISBN: 979-8-35096-659-6

For Kiana, who loves dragons.

Introduction

What is a Dragon Queen?

She's a friend, a sister, a soul mate, a role model, a rebel, an ally, a light, and an inspiration. She's the one who kicks it through the goalpost. Whatever it is, she's on fire; doing her thing like nobody else. Like a boss. Killing it.

...and you want to congratulate her.

Or maybe it's a younger queen who is just starting out in the world and there are things you want her to know.

But sometimes, she's the woman in your life who's holding back, maybe not owning her space. She's someone who has temporarily forgotten her worth, or how to reach for her dreams. Or maybe life has come at her hard and she's hurting. Maybe she's stumbled and can't find her stride. She's unique, beautiful, and capable, but she doesn't feel that way right now. So, you want her to know...

I see you, I value you, I believe in you, and I'm glad you're in my world. YOU are a Dragon Queen.

You command a dragon . . . a creature of great power. That means you will never be alone. You will always be supported, admired and loved...because your dragon is the heart within you, and that fire will never go out.

Note from the Author

This book is dedicated to all my gal pals, my sisters, my soul mates, *my queens*, past, present, and future, who make my life so much better, fuller, more amusing, and more inspirational every day.

I love my Dragon Queens!

This book was never about preaching or perfection. It's about the conversations I believe we all need to have with ourselves, over and over, a thousand times if necessary. I struggle too. I've broken my own rules. There are days when I need to take my own advice. There are times when I fail. There are days when nothing is working, when I don't feel confident, when I'm sad, or I don't have the energy to be my best self. We all feel lost sometimes. Everyone has bad days and I'm no exception, but I don't let myself stay in that place for long. That's when I dig down and call on my inner spirit and have a talk with her.

I call her my dragon.

It's wonderful having a dragon. She's a beautiful, colorful creature with a white, hot flame inside. She can definitely breathe fire! She has scales like armor. She has wicked claws and fangs. She is impossibly strong. She is loyal and wise. She knows me better than anyone and loves me unconditionally. She is a relentless ally. I know she's always there. I can summon her whenever

I need her. When the world feels dark, my dragon is there to protect my heart. She reminds me of all the things I've learned.

> *I've learned* that self-improvement is self-love. We are all worthy of this effort.

> *I've learned* that it's important to check in with myself and find out what I need.

> *I've learned* to feed my spirit by enjoying life, being grateful and leaving room to play.

My dragon reminds me that life is a journey of a million small steps and that every step, even a step backwards, is a lesson. I can choose to believe good things are coming. My dragon's flame will always light my way and guide me back to the path of creating my vision. My dragon fills me with the light of gratitude and makes me strong. She reminds me of who I am and who I'm trying to be, which is...

A person strong enough to love, who is brave enough to try, and who values others.

A person who earns and owns her place in the world, without apology.

A person that I can be proud of.

The best person I can be.

A Dragon Queen.

Dignified.

A Dragon Queen loves herself first.

TO LIVE IN DIGNITY, YOU MUST FIRST TURN YOUR love inward. You must love yourself. If you achieve self-love, your actions and desires will reflect this. Through your decisions and behaviors, you will honor and respect yourself. Your self-respect will inspire you to honor and respect others. That is how you live a dignified life.

Loving yourself first is not a selfish act. It doesn't mean the world revolves around you. It doesn't mean you are better than anyone else. Loving yourself doesn't exclude others. As a beautiful and powerful creature, you have ample reserves of empathy and caring. No one is deprived when you love yourself first.

…but you must learn to love yourself.

It is the foundation upon which your emotional life is built. It will shift the way you view the world. It will change the way you define success. It will determine how you respond to everything that happens to you.

Imagine all the things you might have done differently if you had just loved yourself better.

Without self-love, your dragon will have no flame. Your dragon will shrink and hide in darkness. You must feed your inner dragon with self-love. We all started this journey without skills or experience. Everyone is learning as they go. We make mistakes; some big, some small. People disappoint us; we disappoint ourselves. Some of us feel broken, weighed down by self-doubt or shame.

Look inside, **Dragon Queen.** Your dragon is there. Tell your dragon, *"It's time to wake up. I need you."* Your dragon will remind you that you are a radiant, unique being, worthy of love. You were born that way; you don't have to earn it.

Being worthy of love has nothing to do with accomplishments.

This is hard for accomplished people to accept. It is also hard for unaccomplished people to accept. It isn't the "doing" that makes you worthy of love, simply the "being." Start there.

When you love yourself, your dragon is well-fed and healthy, and her flame is an inferno. Your dragon's fire is an inner strength that will serve you in any situation. You don't have to worry about what is coming; it doesn't matter how challenging it is. When you love yourself, you have the power to meet any difficulty with dignity. You will be able to respond in a way that demonstrates self-love. You will act in a way that is worthy of you. You can

live a life you will be proud of. With a well-fed dragon, you will face the future with courage, and without fear or dread.

So, feel the power within you, **Dragon Queen.** Feed your dragon.

Love yourself.

Reflective

A Dragon Queen knows what she wants.

IT IS THE NATURE OF HUMAN BEINGS TO BE DISSAT- isfied, so everyone wants something. What do you want? Do you want what you have, or do you want something else? What is it? What EXACTLY do you want? It's a very important question. Take the time to think about it. Some people never do.

Be specific. VERY specific. Any goal, no matter how small, should be identified with certainty. Maybe it's a new job or a new relationship. Maybe it's spending more time with your friends or your kids. Maybe it's more money. It can be as simple as finding the time to take a walk every day. Goals are big and small.

What do you want?

People who know what they want, get what they want. Everyone else gets whatever comes to them. Don't limit yourself with fear or doubt or shame.

Imagine what you would do if you knew, without a shadow of a doubt, that your success was guaranteed. If you knew you couldn't fail, would it change your goals?

A **Dragon Queen** spends time on this. She thinks about herself. She questions herself, over and over, because the answers can change when life changes . . . and life is always changing.

When you have your answer, remember that your inner dragon is a vigilant friend. She is very intelligent, and she knows you. She'll insist that you be brutally honest with yourself. She will demand answers. *"You say you want it, but do you really? What does it require? Will it require discipline, more schooling, therapy, a change in lifestyle, or a breakup? Do you want it enough to do what it takes to get there? Don't waste your time serving something that isn't your true desire. Clarify your vision. Is this thing, this goal, this path, what you really want? Are you willing to do what it takes to earn it?"*

The answer might be "no." It may not be something you're willing to do. Saying "no" is not a failure or a flaw; it's a choice. There are many reasons for a "no." Sometimes, we say "no" because it seems like it's just too hard. But your dragon will remind you that *everything* is hard.

Finding a new job is hard. Staying in a job you don't like is hard. Getting paid less than you want is hard. Going back to school to get the job that pays better is hard. Fixing a problem is hard. Dealing with the consequences of not fixing the problem is also hard. *Everything is hard in some way.* No matter what, your choice will be hard. Hard is no excuse.

To get what you truly want, you must be honest with yourself and make thoughtful decisions. If you don't, you will be forced to accept whatever the world throws at you. Maybe you need a change. Maybe you want more. Maybe you're better off right where you are. Only you can answer that.

This isn't about beating yourself up. It's about loving yourself enough to ask the serious questions. It's about making intelligent decisions . . . *honest decisions* . . . ones that you can live with. Questioning yourself is an act of self-love. This is how you feed your dragon.

So, **Dragon Queen,** what do you really want? Think about it. Because you deserve an answer.

Aware

A Dragon Queen is aware of her thoughts and feelings.

HOW CAN YOU MAKE INTELLIGENT DECISIONS ABOUT your life if you don't know yourself? A **Dragon Queen** is mindful. She notices her reaction to the things that happen to her. She identifies her feelings. She respects herself by giving herself permission to feel, and she asks herself why that feeling exists. Anyone can just power through, but most situations don't require that. You can take a minute; you can take a breath.

We are bombarded with stimuli all day long. The competition for our attention is relentless. We are required to know and do in a way that is exhausting. We go, go, go. It's competitive out there. The bar is high for what we consider to be success. It's overwhelming sometimes. How are you doing with it, **Dragon Queen?**

When was the last time you took a moment to check in with yourself? You don't need a spa or a vacation for this. You don't have to be alone, and you

don't need absolute silence. Just pause, take a breath, and say "hello" to your dragon. She will ask . . .

> *"How do you feel right now? Are you hot, cold, tired, or restless? Are you anxious, frustrated, or sad? Do you know why? Would anything help?"*

Sitting with a feeling can be an act of courage. It is also an act of growth. A queen accepts this challenge. She knows that not all feelings require action. You don't always need to release your dragon. Feelings are transient. They may be completely unconnected to what is happening in real-time. Feelings are sometimes a response to something else that happened to us, maybe long ago. Relief might be as simple as acknowledgment...or you might discover a bigger problem, hiding under the surface of your emotions. Feeling it is the only way to know. You can't help yourself if you're oblivious.

Take a minute, maybe several times a day, to stop and take a deep breath. Ask your inner dragon: *"How's it going in there?"* Give yourself permission to feel the answer. Get used to accepting what's happening inside. Acknowledging how you feel is an act of self-love. Honor yourself with this practice. Get to know yourself.

...because you're worth knowing, **Dragon Queen.**

Gutsy

A Dragon Queen is brave.

SHE HAS TO BE. THE WORLD CAN BE A SAVAGE, HEART-less place. It's unimaginable what some people have to endure. Disease, injustice, heartbreak, death...all of them will visit you in some way. The pain they cause can steal your breath away and bring you to your knees. More insidious, but no less dangerous, are fear, loneliness, insecurity, and grief. Persistent and heavy, their weight can drag your spirit down. It can feel like your dragon is drowning. Fear of failure is terrifying in so many ways and the killer of hopes and dreams. We can be so afraid of failure that we get stuck in our uncertainty and lose the courage to try.

No one gets through life unscathed. You will be challenged many times. Your turn is coming. Everyone suffers at some point, some more than others...although comparing levels of pain helps no one. But rest assured that you will be able to meet every challenge with dignity. You will know what to do when an obstacle appears, because YOU are a **Dragon Queen**, and you are brave.

Bravery is not the absence of fear. Bravery is acting with courage and dignity even when you're afraid. It can be hard. Sometimes it's REALLY hard. For some, fighting or retreating feels a lot safer than trying to respond with dignity. But remember, you can DO hard, and you don't have to be alone when you do. There are millions of queens out there, doing their best to be brave, just like you. Find them. Spend time with the women who support and encourage you. Create your "den of dragons." We need our girls, our squad, our besties; the ones we know will always listen and help if they can. They protect our spirit. They feed our dragons.

Don't forget to *look inside.* You have a creature of immense power waiting for your command. She's your inner dragon. When you call to her, she opens her all-seeing eyes. She knows you. She knows how fragile you can be. She knows when you need help. She will say, *"This is a moment of pain. You are suffering. But these feelings are not permanent. They will not destroy you. Remember your spirit. Remember who you are."*

Your dragon will lend you her strength. She will unfurl wings so mighty that they block out the sun. She will flex her deadly claws, ready to do battle against the enemy that threatens you. She has your back. You are not alone.

Your dragon will take a deep breath and ignite the spark that is always alive inside. She will inhale your pain and doubt into her white-hot fire. Her flame fills you with a power so absolute that nothing can resist it. It is the power of self-love. Your dragon will exhale with a deafening roar that clears your mind of all confusion. She will scorch your uncertainty with a blast of fire hotter than a thousand suns. Shame can't survive that kind of heat. Doubt will burn like paper.

You have summoned your dragon. With her, you are mighty. You are capable of winning any battle and defeating any foe. Your dragon's fire will light your path forward. You will never be alone because your dragon is always with you, ready to fight, ready to whisper . . .

"You are worthy. You are loved."

Remember your power, **Dragon Queen.** Call your dragon.

Open-hearted

A Dragon Queen is excited about life.

SHE IS A SEEKER. SHE IS PASSIONATE ABOUT LEARNing. Travel feeds your inner dragon. New experiences keep her flame burning bright. Learn, learn, learn. Read everything. Ask questions. Cherish your curiosity. Try new things. Go places. The world is full of amazing sights, fascinating places, exotic foods, interesting customs . . . and a **Dragon Queen** is curious about all of them.

Experiences are not the only things that feed our dragons. The world is also full of PEOPLE. A queen is constantly meeting new and different people, and she knows the value of a stranger. Each encounter, no matter how brief, is an experience and an opportunity to learn. Especially when those people are different from us.

Not everyone thinks or looks like we do. When you have a well-fed dragon, this is never scary. We can have an open mind. We are safe. We have dragons. We can be kind, respectful and curious with others. This behavior is

necessary for us to live a dignified life. It feeds our inner dragon. It also allows us to feed the dragons in OTHER people.

Every person has an inner dragon. Some of those dragons are very, very small and weak. Their person hasn't provided them with self-love or self-awareness. Their dragon is starving.

But a **Dragon Queen** can feed their dragon through an act of kindness. Kindness can be as small as politely holding a door open. Kindness may mean showing patience when standing in a line or listening to a crying baby on a plane. It can be as simple as a smile. These are little ways to show other people that we see them, that they matter, that they are worthy. This is how we help them love themselves. This is how we feed THEIR dragon.

A **Dragon Queen** loves all dragons. She does her best to feed all of them because no dragon should ever starve. So, when conflict happens, a **Dragon Queen** will remember who she is; a mighty queen worthy of respect, who can bring her dragon's light to the scene. She has many great powers, including confidence and patience. She knows the value of empathy. A queen knows when to take a step back and ask herself . . .

"In this situation, whose dragon needs to be fed?"

Notable

A Dragon Queen knows her worth.

SHE'S NOT AFRAID TO TAKE UP SPACE IN THE WORLD. She knows what she's earned and what she deserves. She is proud of her accomplishments. She has the nerve to ask for what she wants, without guilt, without apology, because she knows that is the only way to get it.

A **Dragon Queen** doesn't wait for success to find her. She knows that to excel, you have to put yourself out there. YOU have to move yourself forward. You have to get in the room. It's entirely up to you. A true queen knows this. She has accepted responsibility for her own success. She knows that no one will come looking for you, no matter what you have to offer, because the world is full of amazing and talented people. You will have to prove yourself. You will have to work hard. You will have to put yourself in the space you want to occupy. You will never be guaranteed a result. You must take the leap and try.

Self-promotion is difficult for many people. We are taught from an early age to hold back when it comes to asserting our worth. Self-confidence has been confused with arrogance.

Promoting yourself is sometimes one of the hardest tests of your self-love. You have to believe in yourself to claim what you want. You have to know that you are worthy if you expect others to believe it too. Self-love is the key to putting yourself out there. If you don't believe in your own worth, you will find ways to sabotage your success. You will find excuses. You will delay. You will make sure you are busy, busy, busy . . . but not in a way that will accomplish your goals.

But you're lucky, because you are a **Dragon Queen**. You can walk into any room with confidence, knowing that you belong there, because you have chosen it. You have fed your dragon. You have self-love. You know that you deserve happiness. You deserve success. You WILL succeed...because how could you fail? When you step up to claim your space, everyone will see...

You've brought a dragon with you.

Qualified

A Dragon Queen has her shit together.

Not every minute of every day, because that's impossible, but she knows what she wants to accomplish and how she's going to do it. A Dragon Queen takes the time to learn the necessary skills. She's prepared. She doesn't pretend to know everything. She is so confident of her intelligence that she doesn't feel embarrassed when she doesn't know something, because she loves herself enough to ask questions and LEARN. A queen honors herself by asking for help when she needs it.

A true queen does her research. She learns what she needs to learn, she practices what she needs to practice, because being unprepared exposes you to failure. Life is hard enough without setting yourself up for a fall. A queen would never disrespect herself that way. It's tricky . . . because our world is always changing. Job requirements change. Technology changes. What we need or want changes. Our abilities change. We are constantly adjusting. So, we're never really done preparing. This is not a problem; it is a reality.

When something unexpected happens, it is easy to be resentful and afraid. We are off-balance. We need time to adjust. This is new territory. We don't know what we're doing.

In that moment, a **Dragon Queen** remembers to first turn her love inward. She remembers to love herself first. She acknowledges the uncertainty. There is no shame in it. She lets herself feel.

Her inner dragon is awake and ready. Her fire is lit, and she is whispering . . . *"You are not the only person who has ever gone through this. You are not the only person who has ever felt this way."* A queen begins to educate herself. She asks . . . *"What is needed here? What are my choices?"* A **Dragon Queen** does her best to create a plan.

In this time of change, her dragon will be at her side, as always. Through every transition, a queen will be warm in her dragon's fire, and together they will light the path ahead.

Unique

A Dragon Queen is extraordinary.

EACH QUEEN IS ONE-OF-A-KIND, UNEQUALED AND unmatched. Some are called different, unusual, eccentric or odd; but these are only words. Better words are . . . original, authentic, interesting, memorable.

Irreplaceable.

...because each queen has her own kind of magic.

The universe craves variety. The world needs diversity. That is why you are here. No one has your exact perspective. You see the world through eyes that are yours alone. Your dragon was formed in the fire of your personal history. You are the sole carrier of your truth. Only by being yourself can you bring something truly unique into the world.

So, be true to yourself. You have talents, great and small. They are yours alone. What can you offer the world? What do you love? What gives you joy? Find your joy. That is where your magic thrives.

Where will you bring your light, **Dragon Queen**?

The world is waiting.

Effective

A Dragon Queen gets it done.

CLEARLY IDENTIFYING A GOAL IS IMPORTANT. BUT once you have your goal, you have to thoughtfully map out the steps necessary to achieve that goal. What do you hope to accomplish this year? This month? This week? Today? Have you asked yourself those questions? It requires time, honest thought, and planning. You won't get there if you don't know the way.

Picture the woman you want to be. Choose your practices, your habits, your routines... and then *show up for them*. A **Dragon Queen** knows that the secret to success is showing up, day after day after day, making slow and steady progress. She will patiently work towards her goal, and when she wanders off course, she will start again; because it isn't all or nothing. Because her dreams are important. Because she is worthy of success. Consistency matters. Chipping away at your goals, checking those little boxes, adds up. Continuous effort pays off.

It's not about living a rigid life. It's about the steps you need to take to make success possible. It's about making the most of your time. Because your time is valuable, **Dragon Queen**.

The clock is ticking, and your dragon is waiting to fly.

Empowered

A Dragon Queen isn't afraid to work.

THEY SAY THAT IF YOU DO WHAT YOU LOVE, YOU will never work a day in your life.

Bullshit. Even if you love what you do, it's still work. You're not sunning by the pool, (unless you're a lifeguard). There will be days when you're tired and you don't want to roll out of bed. You'll have days when you're stuck, and you don't want to do it. There might be times when you actually HATE IT and question every choice you ever made. Those moments are normal and healthy. Everyone gets frustrated. Everyone has a moment of doubt. Nothing worthwhile is easy. To be good at anything you have to put in a lot of effort. You have to work.

A **Dragon Queen** is not afraid of working. She knows that work is not something to be dreaded. It is not an imposition. Work is the pathway to dreams. But even a powerful **Dragon Queen** has bad days, when she's

exhausted and it's hard to get going…or chaotic days, when the excuses pile up…or overwhelming days, when she just wants to roll over, go back to sleep and forget all about it. That's when her dragon will nudge her, and nudge her again if necessary, and remind her … *"Discipline is self-love. You deserve the happiness that reaching your goals will bring you. Everything you do to work towards those goals is an act of self-love. If you can't do it all today, do a little. Do what you can. Some days just showing up, especially when you don't feel like it, is the best way to love yourself.*

So, get up, **Dragon Queen.**

Warm your hands with dragon fire and think about how you can love yourself today. This is how you become the woman you want to be.

Nice

A Dragon Queen is someone you want to know.

SHE'S FRIENDLY AND FUN AND OPEN. SHE'S approachable. No one is beneath her notice.

Children, animals, the elderly, and those with special needs have her special attention and respect. She will look at you when you talk to her. She is present. She listens. She will do her best to give you the time and attention you need. She doesn't pretend she has it all together or that life isn't hard for her too. She isn't afraid to admit that she has faults, because she's always trying hard to improve.

Most of all, a **Dragon Queen** is not entitled. She doesn't believe she is owed special treatment. She doesn't look for someone to blame whenever things go wrong. She is NEVER rude to people working in service industries. Waitstaff, nurses, retail workers, helpline operators, clerks . . . any person who has to serve the public should never be abused. A queen knows that being aggressive and getting loud is NOT the same as confidence. Anyone

can throw a tantrum. Anyone can demand unreasonable things. It doesn't elevate you; it diminishes you. Only the ignorant can't see this. The world doesn't need another bully.

Being rude to someone who is just trying to make a living will cost you your crown.

A queen knows the terrible power she holds inside her and has learned to respect it. Her dragon contains a flame hot enough to melt stone. A queen can scorch the earth with her fury, burn her adversaries to cinders and watch them crumble into dust. But a queen never abuses this power . . . even when she's feeling ignored or disrespected. Her confidence is so solid that she doesn't need to be savage or heartless to claim her place. She has learned that adversity, disappointment, even outrage, can be handled with dignity. She knows that civility is never wasted. It is even more powerful when it isn't deserved.

A true queen has learned that walking away from a situation is sometimes the best way to love yourself. A true **Dragon Queen** saves her dragon's fire for the battles that matter.

Share

LET'S ADD AN "S" TO **DRAGON QUEEN**. IT SHOULD be plural. **Dragon QueenS.** Because there should be more of us.

So spread the word. "S" is for SHARE.

Tap a friend, a co-worker, a neighbor, someone you admire. Maybe you know a young queen who's just starting out in life. This book is one way to tell them...

I see you. I value you. I believe in you.
My life is better because you're in it.
You are a special, unique creature and I think you're amazing. Never lose your swagger. Never lose your sass.
*Never lose that special thing that makes you YOU. Because the world needs you, **DRAGON QUEEN.***

Welcome to the sisterhood.

The Author

CHRISTINE DOWNS is a writer, lawyer, animal-lover, world-traveler, history buff, avid reader, fan of dragons, sci-fi and fantasy, Gemini, enthusiastic wine drinker, amateur sculpture, collector of art and random things, music lover, reluctant cook, aspiring gym rat, Chicago native, dog and cat mom, Los Angeles resident, sarcastic optimist and occasional cynic...and still evolving.

Dragon Queen: a guide is available online at Bookbaby, Amazon, Barnes and Noble, and wherever books are sold.

Please sign up for the newsletter at **hellodragonqueen.com**. Meet other queens and share your advice at **hellodragonqueen** on Instagram or Facebook.